The Path to Soul Immunity

Soul Currency for Life and The Big C with Dr. EB

Published by Impact Publishing®, Lake Mary, FL.

Impact Publishing® is a registered trademark.

Printed in the United States of America.

Text by Autumn Jade Monroe

ISBN: 978-1-7369881-7-6
LCCN: 2022906360

This publication is designed to provide accurate and authoritative information with regard to the subject matter covered. It is sold with the understanding that the publisher is not engaged in rendering legal, accounting, or other professional advice. If legal advice or other expert assistance is required, the services of a competent professional should be sought. The opinions expressed by the authors in this book are not endorsed by Impact Publishing® and are the sole responsibility of the author rendering the opinion.

Most Impact Publishing® titles are available at special quantity discounts for bulk purchases for sales promotions, premiums, fundraising, and educational use. Special versions or book excerpts can also be created to fit specific needs.

For more information, please write:
Impact Publishing®
P.O. Box 950370
Lake Mary, FL 32795
Tel: 1.877.261.4930

The Path to Soul Immunity

Soul Currency for Life and The Big C with Dr. EB

By Best-Selling Author
Sophia Edwards-Bennett, MD, PhD

Impact Publishing®
Lake Mary, Florida

To my daughters,

Satarie and Soferri,

so that they will never forget
the divine legacy of their genealogy:
that the evidentiary probability
of impossibility
is the possibility
of the improbable.

CONTENTS

DEDICATION TO:
MUMMY
SATARIE (THELMA) EDWARDS
(July 15, 1948 – June 28, 1986)
— AMAZING MOTHER OF DWIGHT (TEDDY), ALEXIE
(GARRY) AND ME – (SOPHIA)

How did you do it, Mom?

I can't explain in its entirety
How you coped so gracefully
With all the sticks and stones, words hurled intensely
To break your spirits, and objects to break your bones
   intentionally

Only those who witnessed or experienced firsthand
Could ever narrate, let alone understand
The courage, the faith that one must possess
To not only face each day, but to take the stand
Amidst it all, to help others in need, committing always to lend
   a helping hand
Be it to our extended family, students, colleagues, or the
   stranger - woman or man
What spirit must you have harbored inside
That caliber of person just cannot hide
Not only was there domestic turmoil
There was constant financial deprivation without recoil
Then, like a ripple effect
Your health was attacked too

By your own cells, unable to detect 'who's who'
The downhill spiral of lupus, the trait, the trademark of the
   autoimmune

How did you do it, Mom?

How did you live each day with your head held high,
   shoulders up and heart open wide?
How did you not continuously stumble?
Or curse the hand you were dealt, or grumble?
How is that through all the compounding struggles you didn't
   seem to fumble?
Your actions and words resonated so clearly
That you never stopped believing,
Declaring your faith so adamantly
So, tell me Mom
How did your faith not crumble?

Through it all, you remained so focused on our well being
Instilling a strong foundation of love, faith, will power,
   work ethic, endurance, to name a few
All those priceless intangibles that we could never have
   attained without you
You upheld the tenet of 'do as I say...and as I do'
It was admirable back then and even moreso now in retrospect
Not just to us, as everyone you encountered can attest

Always giving
You treasured the very thought of contributing a morsel of
   pleasure, albeit without measure
And without any expectation of reciprocation of favor

How could you conceive such lofty visions?
Amidst all the poverty, abuse, and endless confusion
You gave us permission to fantasize
To create an ambitious canvas in our minds to visualize
Teddy, Garry, and I were but teenagers then

14

But in the end, decades later, all that you envisioned did
materialize

But I guess you already knew our future reality
Because your faith did not affirm the now in its uncertainty
But in the substance of things hoped for, supernaturally

It's still incredible to think of how
You endured it all, even now
I wonder as I always have, ever since
Even after over three (3) decades since you gained your angelic
wings

My only answer, my only response, my only conjecture...
is that ...
Your love, your patience, your grace, your unrelenting faith,
your heart, your spirit,
Was a thousand-fold more than any planetary wonder
That the mind could ever fathom, even with pensive ponder

Teddy, Garry and I are so blessed, so favored
That you were chosen to be our Mom
And we'll do our best in this world, to pass it along
Admittedly, it's a hard act to follow
But if we can give, love unconditionally, render joy in the midst
of sorrow
Then we know that through us you'll live on, each day, today,
and every tomorrow.

*For I reckon that the sufferings of this present time are not worthy
to be compared with the glory which shall be revealed in us.*
~ Romans 8:18

DEDICATION TO:

KIMBERLY BENNETT-EADY

(December 30, 1979 - August 29, 2021)
— MY SISTER, MY FRIEND and *MYDOCTOREB'S*
Creative UX Designer

Prose for Kimberly's last words:

<u>DON'T WORRY!</u>

Don't worry Kim said
I know this was unexpected
Just like you, I would have loved just a little more time too
Maybe I could have made more lemonade out of limes with you
Because in my life I've had a few (that is …lemons and limes)
Withstanding so many tests of times

Enduring the constantly ferocious intractable pain
But through it all, I must say
That there is a lot that I gained
Insight, wisdom, understanding and patience in life's
    tempestuous terrain
And how did I remain sane?

Well, I was blessed by His Grace
And by you, my genuine friends, and my most dearly treasured
    family
Who loved me so unreservedly and unconditionally

Truth be told
It was on this ever narrowing and winding road
With its twists, turns and sharp bends
That I received the greatest gift of all, as recompense
Because I fell in love with the 'me' within me
The 'me' that shines my light so bright
The 'me with vision
Not just mere sight
The 'me' I pledged that you, the world
And anyone who crossed my path would always see
My heart, my love, yes…all of me
And my proud production: KimberlyBE - Creativity

And yes, the outer shell, my body was ailing
Organs failing fast and faster still
Begrudgingly, all against my will
But courageously, I soared above it
Intentionally, I grew through it
Fiercely, I forged beyond it
Gracefully, I lived in spite of it
I battled, I fought relentlessly
And now, I'm finally free from it

And
I know you'll query
Why did I have to go?
But don't worry
I just have a 'head start' to a better place
Filled with His splendor, Glory and only because of His
    amazing Grace

But I'll meet you there some day
Where all fears are allayed
And there, we'll spill 'all the beans' we didn't say
We'll laugh out loud

We'll reminisce
And you'll tell me all the treasured moments that I missed
You'll remind me of how much wit I evinced
And then confess that you haven't laughed that hard ever
    since...

Oh, and there's one more thing
I'll be watching
So don't forget my styling tips
And remember, my usual advice,
No hard swings
Just gently sway those hips

So, until then
You have all the memories we made, and all the ones we
    penned
All the laughs, and the crazy things we did back then
All those moments
The big ones, the little ones and the in-between too
And whenever you think of these memories there'll be a
    twinkle, then a smile
Just remember, that's me reminding you

Don't worry
For I'm at peace on the other side
Don't worry
I'll see you again, in the sweet by and by.

Lesson learnt from my Fathers about Second Chances

The fruits of second chances: Exhibit A - presented in the courtroom of judgement or condemnation, serves as substantiating evidence for forgiveness, undeniably irrefutable even by the strongest prosecutor's closing remarks to the contrary.

I learnt this lesson from my earthly father Rupert Emmanuel Edwards, and my Heavenly Father Emmanuel (God with us).

⤙ *Preface* ⤚
to
PART A

Why Me?
Why you?

I wrote this book
To be obedient to His command
Because He deposited within me a decree of soul
  demand

And without a doubt I do believe
He gave me vision so that I could see
That there is someone who really needs to receive
These blessed words
To neutralize internal conflicts, seeking reprieve

Someone who is in dire need
To be told, to hear or to read
This book's contents, and to digest
Whether now, by introspect
Or in the future, in retrospect

So think of this as a colloquy
For anyone who, in your darkest hours, has asked the
  question "why me" repeatedly
The little boy or girl in the midst of, or reliving in your
  mind, childhood trauma
The boy, the girl, the woman, the man who feels
dejected
Having lost count of how many times you've felt
rejected

For you, the abandoned
For reasons unfathomed

For the hurt and abused
Alone and confused
For all the misfits, labeled 'different'
Yearning to be accepted
For the insecure, for whom to belong is the allure
Or for the gifted
Arrested in your potential
Not revealing your best
Lest you be seen as an imminent threat

For the chosen, called to manifest your purpose, ordained divinely
But deep down you harbor feelings of inadequacy

Or maybe you're afraid that if you dare to soar
You'll be met with unsolicited abhor

This book is for you
If you're at a crossroad
Where the paths ahead you do not wish to trod or take
And everything around you spells confusion
And sense of it all, try as you may, you cannot make
Maybe you feel trapped in a reality that you can't escape
And after all the energy expended is sapped
After the sweat of your brows, master-minding and overworked hands
Nothing in your present or future looks even vaguely similar to the life you planned
And it seems you are swiftly sinking in quick sand
Your mental skyscrapers are all leveling to the ground
And for all your lofty dreams and aspirations

Not a mustard seed of hope can be found

Maybe....
You ask yourself, *"Why me?"*
Repeatedly....

Because it seems nothing ever goes right
And, with one disappointment after another
Your days are as dark as your nights
And there's no sense in hoping for tomorrow

So with your mind embracing this narrative
You decide there's no use crying
And, your internal soliloquy echoes in affirmation
There's no need trying

This book is for you
If you're falling deeper into the chasm of isolation
Drowning in hopelessness and depression
So much so that if someone throws you a rope
You pause and think
You're reticent, scared to trust again, or hope
Because you dread the familiar cycle
That cycle of hope, later replaced by the bitter taste of
     disappointment
Over and over and over again

So you wrestle in your mind
As the strength you struggle to find
To seize that rope
To hold on to hope, just one more time

You see
The question *"why me"?*
Is surrounded and confounded by any and all
     circumstances, past or contemporary
It underscores or intimates what, where or who, in
     the present you don't want to be

And since your past or your present provides
no impetus to be otherwise inclined or project
optimistically
You foresee an immutable unfavorable future,
inevitably

Here's the salient truth that I humbly proclaim
But first, allow me to disclaim:
That I, by no means self-acclaim
To be a sage or all-knowing czar

Herein I simply share my revelation
Hoping that in its dissemination
The wisdom it imparts, raises the bar
Of our understanding and elevation

So, with hearts wide open, or at least ajar
I beseech you to receive this ensuing statement that
I avow
Sincerely, and with deepest regard

*'Your present is not your past; your future is not
your present'*
Stated blandly
Is deceptive in its seeming simplicity
But is profound if examined keenly
Understood completely
And embraced with intentionality

You see…
The past should not govern in the present
No matter how painfully similar the circumstances
of their respective existence
And by said argument, your present is not your
future, albeit in chronological sequence
Regardless of the bleak days or raging storms
Or blatant oppression fueling recurrent feelings of

deep depression
I know a blink of light can be outcast by the darkness
from the past and all its frustration
But if you look ahead, there's a constant flicker of
light in the future, coupled with an invitation

I know you must be thinking...

For one:
'Sounds like a cliché'
Or
'Easier said than done'

But for all of us, the truth we believe
Whatever thoughts occupy and dominate our
mental 'real estate' at any moment in time
Profess to be our perpetual reality
For that is, for better or worse, the power of the
mind

But may I contend from experience
And thus, emboldened with confidence
That who you were, is not who you are
And who you are while you still breathe
Indeed....
Is not who you were created to be
So, the 'who' that you will be
Has yet to be revealed

But what matters, what's irrevocably true
For everyone, including you
Is the actual path from our past to our present, and
the road to our future
Because it is the journey, that germinates the
commixture of nature and nurture
Whether balanced or skewed, it's the ultimate
instructor
Because it's on that journey that you'll discover

Who you are, who you are not
What's important, what's true
What - to you - means little, and what means a lot
And all the truths in between to discover
Not about annals, or the current era
Not about status, beliefs or profession
Not about decadent, vestige, or existing culture

But instead, the truth about you, this unique,
    exquisite creature
To whom the omnipotent, omniscient one
The progenitor of creation
With His Glory and splendor
Granted this incredible gift of life
In all His sovereignty and providential pleasure

Because within you, there's a pilot light
That even in the darkest of night
Awaits that match to strike
And with just a flicker, convert to a flame that's
    perpetually bright

So, through the triumphs and failures,
Through storms, sunshine and rain
Serenity or indescribable pain
In moments of darkness or contentment
There's a diametric sojourn of enlightenment
Envisioned with an assigned mission
To shed the lies, the fallacy of false narratives
Stripping away the layers, the dissimulate
    superlatives
Peeling away the 'veneers' you've amassed
Uncovering the deceitfully tasked, masquerading
    mask

Until, alas, you gain the vision
With insightful discernment
Illuminated by His light

Hold on desperately to that vision
Don't let it leave your sight
Because that vision is the emissary
The ambassador for your mission

It's the first aid kit of Hope
That will sanitize the wound of sorrow
That will bandage the laceration of desolation
Heal the broken heart from the depths of depression
To revive a life of promise
So that your eyes will see in the distance of
    tomorrow
That fire, that light, or even just that flicker
To hope for a brighter future

To observe the reflection of your divine dimensions
The acreage, the ambits of your potential
The revelation of you in totality

Then, and only then, retrospectively
Will you finally appreciate your journey

The unedited, uncut past, present, and into the future
    unquestionably

So that, when you ask yourself the question, *"why
me"*?

You'll respond without refrain, unequivocally

"The only human being I ever want to be
Is the beautiful soul that He created for His
    Kingdom, in his infinite wisdom
So, with intentionality, I will be
The, bold, the brave, the inimitable *'me'*"

⋙ PART A ⋘

The discovery of the light bulb was borne from the evolution and collation of concepts, experimental trials and many failures. Fruition and success required the cognitive prowess and perseverance of many scientists; from Alessandro Volta in Italy, to Humphrey Davy in Great Britain, to British Scientist Warren De la Rue, to Bowman Lindsay, to the English Physicist Joseph Swan. All synchronously with, and ensued by, Thomas Edison's thousands of attempts to finally produce the incandescent light bulb. And even then, the light bulb required the enlightenment of Lewis Howard Latimer, who discovered the essential fiber filament.

A priori, lessons were learnt from each predecessor's experiences
    and discoveries
And as a result, the incandescent light bulb was auspiciously
    transposed from a cerebral concept to its existence in the
    earthly realm
Subsequently, from the light bulb, countless new discoveries
    have been gained
With, undoubtedly, even more in the future attained

The lesson from this historical perspective is that:
Though our experiences may be different

Whether stationed remotely, or in close proximity
We can all learn from the collective narratives of our buffet of
   life processes

From our Ecclesiastes
And by that, I mean...
Our failures, how we rebound
Our adversities, how we rise and abound
Our pain, how we heal
The decisions we make
Those in which we partake
The ones from which we refrain
The appeals we heed and the desires we feed

After all, we are all connected
Temporally, relatively or annexed through yet undefined circuits
   or cyber interconnectivity

So in **Part B** of this book, in which I share my journey with you...
Or in **Part C**, where I highlight the sojourn of cancer patients
   and their loved ones too
Both explore, *highlight* and impart
$oul currency that can be espoused in all walks of life
Applied in challenging seasons, life crises, life-threatening
   illnesses or otherwise

To extrapolate, to glean, to recognize
That though we're all different and unique
That whatever paths we may trod or seek
Though admittedly not the same
One thing's for sure
And that is, we all face pain

So, **Parts B** and **C** should not be distinct or isolated
But instead, should be collaboratively masticated, digested and
   assimilated
To concentrate all the lessons, the stories, the proses that speak
   so incisively to you

To lend a voice to your thoughts, the things you do not say
To allay doubts, that linger from day to day
To debunk the fable of indestructible giants that you think
cannot be slayed
To disarm the battle of wills perceived as insurmountable hills
To dismantle the fears you harbor inside
About the mountains that you decide are too impossible for you
    to climb

This collective probing expatiate is meant to penetrate your
    spirit, your soul, your inner being
To excavate those hidden treasures
The yet untapped, the unmeasured
That which you never knew was dormant inside you
The seeds planted over the course of your life
Germinating, budding, blooming sequentially
The experiences that marinate, and effuse an aroma of wisdom,
    so boldly

So that in time
Through your own revelatory experiences, you will amass
A rich, seasoned elixir of $oul currency
And alas... maybe
You'll record your own odyssey
Your bridges, your hurdles, your victories

Your journey
To Soul Immunity.

The Psychological Soundtrack of a Cancer Patient

♪ *THIS ONE'S ON YOU* ♪

None of this seems real
My mind, my thoughts, my will, are all grappling to appeal

Blindsided by the unexpected, from out of left field

I'm shocked, I'm bewildered, I'm numb
I can feel my heart pounding in my chest
Vibrating like a cymbal, staccato like a drum
Piercing through this awkward silence
The solemness from a bottomless pit

It is so loud, doesn't anyone hear it?

I was fine
Albeit, far from perfect
But I was living a life that I thought was mine
But now it doesn't align
With what I'm facing
This diagnosis-this Big C
I'm gravely fearing

I'm pacing
I can't sit still
I peer through the blinds
Resting my elbows on the windowsill
My eyes are open, but they don't register much of anything
Because my mind is so clustered
I'm patently flustered
Ruminating, grappling with the news
I'm shocked and confused

What does this all mean?
For me, my life, loved ones, or my family?
Because this reality

Is not in synchrony
With what I thought life had in store for me
What my present or future would be
Because just a few days ago, I was basking in a different reality

So, I'm solemnly asking
What does this mean?
Because there are so many things I haven't done, haven't seen
Goals unfulfilled; places I haven't been

NO...NO!!
It never occurred to me
That this could possibly be my reality
I planned my life's itinerary-so meticulously
Best laid plans
I never thought I'd be dealt this fateful hand

Then, sighing heavily
I breathe in deeply

Settling my mind into my present reality
Deep thoughts, weighted on the beam balance of uncertainty
Catalogued with intensity

I say to myself
As if to spiel in unison
Ok...shake it off
Man up: This is not the time to be emotionally soft
Or: Woman, be bold, be brave, you're strong
I know your path in this life has been rather arduous and long

Willing my thoughts and emotions to rein in
Eyes looking up, I question him
Lord, is this a test?
Should I, as they say: "forget the rest and hope for the best?"

Then, a voice from the back of my mind's pew
Responds right on cue

This one, this time, this affliction, this battle, this kind is new
I'm scared, restless
Confused and defenseless
For there is nothing in my power that I can do
So, all I can say is:
God, this one's on you.

◎ THE NAKED TRUTH ◎

Walking in my patients' shoes

Can you imagine one day, which started just like any other day. You wake up, reviewing in your mind, like the reels of a cassette player, the expected, the planned, the anticipated tasks for the next few minutes, the next few hours at hand. With its routine, the hustle, the bustle, the deadlines, the 'to do list' you desired to accomplish. Or maybe it's a usually quiet and peaceful morning, predictable in its rote consistency.

Then, just one moment, one conversation, one call, one voicemail, one envelope in the mail, one confirmed suspicion, shatters your entire preserved, stable, dependable safe pedestrian normalcy.

You're rendered a diagnosis that, although the details are unknown, you know that it could threaten your very existence.

Then, hosting this knowledge in your mind in incremental moments each day thereafter; it festers, propagating more ponder, perseveration of an entire suite of emotions. A panoply of rapid-fire thoughts and unanswered questions conceived, as the negative outcomes you perceive. Ruminating, on fast forward, the stark possibility that you may leave your loved ones and family members.

Fear, cohabitating with anxiety. That is a feeling that is indescribable, a fear that is incomprehensible. Even though we know *momemto mori*, that we are mortal beings on this earth for an appointed time only. This awareness does not negate the shock, like a painful dagger in one's heart. The intensely piercing pain, a hollow space where a deep and gaping chasm of uncertainty remains.

This is just a forensic glimpse into the psychological binge, the malady of the mind of a patient who has been diagnosed with the

Big C, cancer. This narrative is akin to an emotional arrhythmia; it vacillates. Then, like a scratched vinyl record on replay, it insidiously escalates at the time of diagnosis (but often persists during treatment and thereafter).

Then ensues the barrage of multiple consultations, serial imaging studies and formulation, curated and conveyed instructions for the recommended treatment algorithms – much of which, falls into a mental abyss of the bewildered, upheaved state of mind. Nonetheless, amidst the haze of dismay, survival instincts prevail, and, though not anesthetizing, incite the decision to pursue cancer therapy.

The Limitations of Tradition

The approach of traditional medicine includes: the acquisition of information, analysis, outcomes, and application of level 1 medical research evidence.

It is contemporarily relevant, indubitably essential and clinically effective. Thus, as is implicit in my educational background and training, and explicit in my daily oncological practice, I am complicit in the utilization of evidence-based, effective, multimodality treatment.

As such, I utilize all my expertise, acumen, knowledge acquired, and every resource in my armamentarium to treat every patient, always seeking to produce an outcome beyond/better than predicted, for any given site or stage of disease.

However, in my fifteen (15) years in practice, I've witnessed another type of tumor.

That which synchronously arises with the diagnosis of cancer. The invisible tumors.

I speak of the psychological tumors:

Crippling doubts
Paralyzing fears
Cascading tears
Restless anxieties
Incarcerating hopelessness
Mortified spirits

Thus, even when the desired cancer treatment response is attained, i.e., treatment is successful, the remnant tumors linger. There are ebbs and flows, rising within unpredictable moments, exposing more wounds including, but not limited to, the plaguing, nagging fear of the knowledge of possible future recurrence.

So, while traditional medicine has established its protocol for
    the gross physical tumor, the cancer
There is no standard operating procedure for the invisible
    tumors unveiled herein
No, there is no guaranteed treatment algorithm for the
    hemorrhaging of hope
No, there is no established cure
No effective regimen, no concoction, cocktail, or connoisseur

And while appropriate counseling referrals can be ventured, they are often not utilized for several reasons including but not limited to: stigma, time-consuming cancer treatment schedule, (as explored in my prior book *"Higher Ground"*).
So then, what is the antidote?
How do we attack these invisible tumors?
To heal the wounds of the soul that are open, even when the physical wounds have been closed.

◎ <u>911</u> ◎

This is the 911 call within our medical field
To treat not just the body
But to address the hearts, minds, and souls of our patients

Yes, there is a 911 reckoning
Not just to listen to their beckoning

But to hear what our patients do not say
The encrypted thoughts they are reticent to convey
To see the vulnerability, they do not wish to reveal
To be used as a vessel, a channel, a conduit to heal
To penetrate their sorrow
To provide a cable of hope for tomorrow
To caress their pain
To resuscitate their hearts
To inoculate their fears
To infuse in their minds that hope lingers near
To excavate the yet untold
The hidden wounds of their anguished souls

To answer this call, I believe that we must expand our current
    practice of medicine.
We must radicalize our traditional, standard operating
    procedures.
To institute one that transcends the normal, the usual,
    traditional pathways
To establish the capstone of our clinical architectural blueprint
To define the contextual framework

This institutional upgrade is necessary because:
The deep wounds of the heart
The deep well of hopelessness
The deep pit of despair

Requires a divine deep dive into the Ministry of Medicine:

- *To enter Intercession*
- *To render Impartation*
- *To confer Revelation*
- *To offer Restoration*

Partnering with the Divine is free, no health insurance required, no deductibles apply.

For example, when we corral the presence of a Chaplain for our patients in their passing, and their family members, to invoke quietude and solace; our patients and their loved ones invariably welcome this intervention.

Thus, in addressing a facet of the Ministry of Medicine, i.e., intercession, allow me to introduce this proposal in question:

Can we repurpose such invocations to add to our psychological toolbox?

Can we expand the parameters of our therapy by employing a more systemic intercessional approach during treatment, at our patients' and their loved ones' discretion?

Could this proposed intervention function as a hub of support, comfort, spiritual engagement and enrichment?

In full disclosure, with my patients, given permission or overt invitation
I engage in spiritual conclave and prayer, resulting in much soul luminosity, by their admission

To be clear, the proposed does not require a diametric paradigm shift from the dogma of traditional doctrines and clinical methodologies. It is not meant to discard, but to include, to expand, to enhance. Thus, one does not preclude the other.

Just as we utilize a multidisciplinary approach resulting in multimodality cancer treatment by employing surgery, chemotherapy, and radiation therapy for cancers such as brain, head and neck, lung, breast, colorectal cancers, to name a few.

It is equally plausible to enhance traditional cancer care by the application of a therapy 'beyond the body', thus treating the mind, body and soul.

To Institute Change in Institution:

Requires a protocol, a path, a currency in some format, and protection, guarantee, security, i.e., a form of immunity.

Herein, the path proposed, themed and titled, involves the *currency* of the *Soul. A posteriori*, it is relevant to explore the meaning of these terms literally and contextually.

◎ DEFINING SOUL, IMMUNITY AND CURRENCY ◎

What is the Soul?

The soul is described as:
The spiritual part of a human being.
The emotional intensity or energy.

What exactly is Immunity:

Medical experts report that there are three (3) types of Immunity:

Innate, Adaptive and Passive.

Innate means to be born with.

Adaptive means developed with, and by, the body's immune system in response to exposure to an antigen.

Passive immunity is immunity that results from the introduction of antibodies from another person or animal.

The role of the immune system is:
1) To fight disease-causing germs like bacteria, viruses, parasites or fungi, and to remove them from the body.
2) To recognize and neutralize harmful substances from the environment.
3) To fight disease-causing changes in the body, such as cancer cells.

Herein, I focus on:

Adaptive immunity: Adaptive (or active) immunity develops throughout our lives.
In the context of this book, adaptive immunity is analogous to soul immunity.

Passive Immunity: Immunity that results from the introduction of antibodies from another person or animal.

In the context of this book, passive immunity represents the impact of others in our lives. I regard such people as *"Divine,*

Disguised and Dispatched", placed in our lives at important junctures to facilitate our passage to purpose, and our path to Soul Immunity.

How do we define Currency?

Currency is defined as: a resource or means of exchange for tangible or intangible products.

We usually think of currency as associated with a monetary or financial value, a tangible source. However, in this context, currency is an intangible, yet valuable element employable in life.

It's the essentials, the factors, the elements that we need to find the exact coordinates in the corridors of our minds, to address the deficits, the insufficiencies, the insecurities, the fears, the anxieties, the pain, and the wounds from which our invisible trauma originates. It is not superficial but seeds deep. That is, $oul currency.

As it is with the deposit of monetary currency, so it is with soul currency. The form of deposit varies, depending on the source, and that accepted by the entity or person in receipt. As with any deposit, state (as opposed to estate) value increases for the receiver. However, in the case of $oul currency, the value of the grantor does not decrease.

A priori, $oul currency, though intangible, has the potential to increase the value of the receiver and the grantor; the effect, albeit intangible, and thus immeasurable.

This $oul currency transaction described above, could be considered a currency exchange. For example, if one offers $oul currency such as encouragement, the receiver gains hope or courage. The grantor may gain fulfillment or joy as a response to the receipt or gain of another.

As it is with different regions of the world, we all have different ilks of currency. Some shared or the same. Others unique, with dynamic exchange rates.

Exchange can occur under different circumstances, such as is required for monetary currency in the setting of a travel venture to a different country. Regardless of the exchange rate, the transaction is essential to acquire the currency necessary for use in that specific country.

Thus, $oul currency exchange is vital for all the aforementioned reasons. In fact, there is multiplicity. In that, encouragement rendered, lends further encouragement to encourage others.

As with financial currency, $oul currency has the capacity to change one's status.

In this case, currency can alter one's status; or more appropriately ascribed, one's state of mind, spirit or penetrable soul. Utilizing the example above, encouragement can change a discouraged state of mind, a depressed spirit or a despondent soul.

As you progress throughout this book, you will encounter numerous $oul currencies. Some innate, some taught or deposited, others garnered from experiences; whether adverse or positive.

Why is this important in your life or mine?

Well, we all individually, and collectively, have and need $oul currency. And, as I purport, it is the cynosure, a lifeguard, to soul immunity.

Likened to the human interconnecting framework of our lymphatic and immune system; as we accumulate $oul currency amidst, within, and through life experiences, each subsequent battle, adversity or unexpected emergency, is faced with increasing equanimity. Indeed, that is the undeniable experiential, evidential and incremental gain in the strength, vigor and range of one's soul immunity.

This concept applies throughout this book. The acquisition of $oul currency, bolsters one's resilience; fortifying one's soul immunity.

In *Part B* of this book, I highlight timelines, milestones, and experiences in my life, during which I, introspectively or in retrospective, gained $oul currencies. Aggregately, these intangibles guided me on my path to soul immunity.

You may ask, imbibed with curiosity:

How is $oul currency and/or immunity relevant to a cancer patient, their loved ones, or the medical community at large?

The answer is the incessant 911 call: to treat not just the body. But to address the hearts, minds and souls of our patients.

By impartation, intercession, revelation and restoration through The Ministry of Medicine.
Disseminating $oul Currency.
Demarcating a Path to Soul Immunity

Thus, in *Part C* of this book, I focus on cancer patients and their loved ones. I employ proses and interludes. From their titles and contents, $oul currencies and a path to soul immunity can be discerned and delineated respectively.
To illuminate a *Path to Soul Immunity*.

Herein I offer to you, what I deem as Dr. EB to be, *$oul Currency for Life* and the Big C.

⤜ *Preface* ⤛
to
PART B

If I composed an account of my story
My path to soul immunity, which I am still
   sojourning
From birth to date would be Sisyphean
Entailing the sum tribute of a plethora of my life's
   resumes
Quilted with minutiae and repurposed threads
So instead, I've decided to share just a few allegories
   of my experiences
Which served dual purposes
Catharsis and metamorphosis
The experiences that wounded but grounded
Those by which I was daunted but also inculcated
Those that against me seemed to conspire
But by which my faith was even more inspired
Those I so adamantly fought
But indelible lessons they consistently taught
Those that broke me
Yet stronger I was made to be
Those that haunted, taunted me repeatedly
So much so that I was desperate, compelled by grace
   to break free
And in doing so, gained $oul currency
Leading to, building, cultivating and strengthening
   my soul immunity

45

⤜ PART B ⤛

⤙ *Prologue to Part B* ⤚

Some wounds healed, but forever scarred
Innocence unwittingly marred

Some bruises raw
Nursed with the proverbial icepack until thawed
But nonetheless, there's a story that's being told
In, and between, the lines of each prose
Intricately woven in
Amidst the rhymes and rhythms
But it's all there…
Forayed in the tone and the cadence implicitly
And, if you read carefully
You'll detect the salient words placed or misplaced
   deliberately.
 For their meanings to be interpreted craftfully

So, as we proceed
Allow me to concede
To the maker, the breaker and the mender
The keeper, the protector of my soul
In this, ***Part B***'s, introductory prose.

⚘ *GRACEFULLY BROKEN* ⚘

Full of anguish, rebirthing pain
Rejected, retorted with disdain
Defensive alerts from all the past hurts

Should, could, would I ever be
Acknowledged, or at least accepted, for simply being me

Cursed by the misconceptions or misconstrued perception
Through the lens of ferocious competition
Or resented for my coat of one color
Sometimes minutes, sometimes endless hours

If only they knew my heart, my intentions
The nights of never-ending ruminations
How long they last
The untold past
The feuds, the observed and inflicted abuse
The peril that lingered in my mind, hurt and confused
The battles I fought and still fight
Day and night
The scars injured anew
The insecurities that woo
Oh, if only they knew

But, at each juncture when hope was almost erased
When I thought refuge, or security
At least, for me, was not to be
The disguised, He dispatched divinely
To reassure, to guide, to support, to love, and encourage,
    ever so unselfishly
To remind me that He honors His promise, He hears our inner
    plea, and renders mercy, ever so faithfully

Though imperfect, humanly fallible
Unrecognizable to myself, and in my assessment, to Him

His abiding light never once grew dim
Not with condemnation, but instead Grace, He reciprocated as
  recompense

The sufferance, the pain, the ups and downs
The laughter, the tears and the frowns
He was there through it all
Looking down,
To soothe my sorrow
From his diadem – his heavenly crown

You see …
In this odyssey of my life, He was teaching me
Who I was really meant to be
That the light I could not see
Was the light within me
And once I discovered the truth
It did indeed, set me free

For growth and enlightenment
And mindful ascent
To another cerebral stratum
He provided the dimensions
From fleeting fundamentals
To profound ponder
All gifts of His Grace and marvelous wonder

So broken I was, yet He carried me
Through the loss, the rejections, the maze and the pain
And all that occurs in life's unpredictable terrain
And when life brings the unexpected
Broken again I'll probably be
But I know now, that my Savior
He carries me
By Him I was created, exquisitely made
So I won't be afraid
Because he knows every gray and white matter in my brain

Every organ, every tissue plane, every nerve, every artery and
  every vein
He knows every joint, every bone within me
So whatever life brings, as I was then, so I will be
Carried, while I'm being **broken, gracefully**

My brethren, count it all joy, when ye fall into diverse temptations;
  knowing this, that the trying of your faith worketh patience.
    But let patience have her perfect work, that ye may
      be perfect and entire, wanting nothing.
        ~ James 1: 2-4

◎ THE CORRIDORS OF TIME ◎

The effusive emotions, uncertainty, confusion, anxiety and
despair highlighted in the prose, in **Part A** entitled "This One's
on You", though contextually distinct, are reminiscent of my
inner persistent tug of war after losing my mother to lupus at
such a tender age. From 8-13 years old, I vividly recall our
(my brothers Dwight aka Teddy, Alexie aka Garry, and me)
understated, tenuous existence, my mother's life-threatening,
overwhelming, weakening, recurrent lupus flares, sequential
loss of multiple organ functions, numerous hospitalizations and
her ultimate transition.

To Live Another Day

It was that dreadful night that was far from bliss
Correction, not night, dark – in the fourth watch – before break
of dawn, morning dew or mist
After Mom (or Mummy as we called her), had undergone surgery
Pronounced stable for discharge
She came home that day, on the road to recovery
At least that's what we hoped, optimistically

I recall as if it was yesterday, that night there was rain, lightning
    and thunder
So, we all fell into deep slumber
But, a few hours later
We were awakened by our mom's groaning and incoherent
    mutter
In that moment, I can't recall what we said, or what was uttered
But what we saw, our reaction could not be tempered
Mummy was laying in blood
But my 9-year old mind in irrational denial registered a flood
As I recalled the leaky zinc roof, amplifying the pouring rain's
    pitter-patter
And the frightening lightening and thunder

But in reality,
Mummy was the one wet, cold and clammy
And although none of us dared to voice our thoughts openly
We all feared the worst was fast approaching, imminently

But paralyzed by our fears, we couldn't be
She needed medical attention emergently
We knew that calling for an ambulance in Jamaica was futile,
and would not be addressed promptly

Furthermore, we had no mode of telecommunication
And to add to our calamity, we had no method of transportation
At least, not at Nana's (our great-grandmother's) abode, where we
were staying, in the country-side, which was quite remote

But in that desperate moment, we thought of a family friend,
    Mr. Green, who owned a funeral home, and a hearse, who
    resided a few miles away
A hearse, morbid, I know
But that was the least of our worries, on that night, pending the
    break of day
Hearts pounding, our mother though in pain, weakly muttering
But I recognized, though faint, that she was praying

My brothers ran to Mr. Green's home in the dark, in the pouring
  rain
Propelled by the image of Mummy, bleeding, writhing in pain
After what seemed like forever
They arrived with Mr. Green at the steering wheel of the hearse
No one spoke as we drove to Linstead Hospital
As dreadful, unfathomable thoughts in our minds we rehearsed
But Mummy's fervent faith, pierced through the silence
While questions raced in our minds, anxious lips pursed

We arrived at the hospital and she was rushed into surgery,
immediately
Thankfully, without complications, she emerged
She was stabilized, and returned home, again
Saved, to live another day
To guide us, to teach us, all that her faith empowered her to say
To utter, to impart more nuggets of wisdom
To live each day as a statement of Grace, faithfully serving in
  His Kingdom

⟩ *RELENTLESS FAITH* ⟨

Even with her progressive illness and challenges

Mummy made so many sacrifices
She harbored so much faith, and demonstrated so much grit
I recall the days she didn't eat
So that we could stay nourished
The boxes of disposed loose paper she procured
Traveling from Linstead to Kingston via 'River Road' and many
  detours
All this effort just to secure
Staple and compile 'makeshift' composition books that we
  could not otherwise afford

And how could I forget the restless nights which steadily grew,
  engulfed by fear

As the tumultuous and turbulent domestic affairs
Saturating our minds with endless tension
Predicted that a pernicious imminent traumatic ending was near
Grim, right?
Would we ever see anything closely resembling light
The investment in time, man-hours of teaching, knowledge
    attained
The intellectual ability our Mom fought so diligently to sustain
Didn't seem to matter anymore
All of that pain, seemingly without gain
Drought after drought for life is all my brothers and I could
    foresee
As our Mom, our hope for survival
Lying in the hospital bed
Clinging to life herself
Light ahead-some said?
In this life?
No, there was only darkness at best
Emotionally intoxicated with hopelessness
But Our Mom, Satarie Edwards, affectionately called Thelma
She had a mountain of Faith
The size of a mustard seed was far too little, in her humble
    opinion, she would adamantly state
Inciting a strong rebuttal, a debatable contest
Because what she foresaw for our lives, even in death
Would have been rightfully refutable
An argument, that given the evidence, would be circumstantial
    at best.

𝄞 *UNCONDITIONAL HOPE* 𝄢

But here we stand today
To anyone who will listen, we say
The desperation, the life of despair
The future you fear
As irrevocable or real as it may seem

Could colossally change
Could be remarkedly different, divinely arranged

Understandably, if you declared victory in your deprived stage
You would seem utterly deranged

But I challenge you
To speak, to see, to hope anew
And pray that your faith, you will renew

Because as much as you planned
Carefully mapped and plotted with your mind and penned with
    your hands
You must admit
That this life, what's occurring even now, you could not predict

For none of us have even the slightest clue what the future holds
And admittedly, we all passionately dislike not having complete
    control
But we can only see 'what gives' as we live
And as this life continues to unfold.

◎ <u>LESSONS TO GO</u> ◎

Addressing Trauma, Loss and Grief

With so many sequential haunting challenges
There was no time to process the emotional lacerations, let
    alone heal
Survival mode was the dominant force that propelled us on our
    course
There was simply no time to appeal

But at some juncture, some moment in time unforeseen,
    unannounced and unexpectedly
Whether triggered or dictated by accumulation to the brink, the
    threshold of psychological or emotional capacity

The violations, the unaddressed trauma
Emotional wounds inflicted, no matter how long ago
They resurface with repercussions, like a relentless haunting foe
And with bulwark, barricading woe

Take residence, establishing strongholds

The psychological damage, that suffocating, stifling, relentless
    kind
Allows no room for denial or a seat at the back row of one's
    mind
But to heal requires 'facing the music' with unreserved
    acceptance
With or without acknowledgement of the accused or
    perpetrator's repentance
Regardless of paid penance, voluntary admission or reformation

So, I couldn't and would never have healed
But for the altar at which I surrendered and finally kneeled
This burden, to Him, I wholly and resolutely, had no choice but
    to yield.

The Soul of the Process

So, what lessons did I learn?
What wisdom did I earn?
What knowledge did I gain?
Or select paths or pitfalls from which to refrain?

The lessons were interspersed
Some inserted insidiously and slowly
Others with a sudden burst

But it's really the process that matters, ultimately
For it's the journey that yields $oul currency

Allow me to expound for your clarity.

You see...
During adversity
The moments, the fears you incur as your thoughts you dissect
While you mull over the myriad of choices, the outcomes you
    project
As the emotions and swirling doubts cycle through your mind
The ebbs and flows
Peaks and troughs
The vicissitudes of life
Can, and some will, inevitably be unkind

Life is akin to a psychological assembly line
That demands the protocol specifications for the destiny of time
But it is in this jolting period of uncertainty, the unanswered
    questions flooding our minds
That our soul and spirit are exposed
To the renewal, the evolutionary processes
The mitosis and the angiogenesis

The incubation and the gestation
The labor; the crowning and the birthing

The growth and the training
The percolating and distilling

The sifting and refining
The groaning and atoning
The curation and the graduation
The renovation and maturation
The reconditioning and rehabilitation
The anchoring and stabilization

Yes, it's all occurring through life's treacherous terrain
But at times we're so blinded by the struggle, the hurt and pangs
    of deep pain
We're so disoriented by serial adversities
So much so that we don't pause to embrace it; or be edified by
    the sage lessons in it

But if we endure, take courage and live through it
The renewed you emerges on the other side, as it was for
   Joseph, after he was thrown by his brothers in the pit
For indeed, it is in the threshing, the pruning, the making after
   the breaking
It is in the catharsis, that true evolution exists, and
   transformation persists
Thus revealing one's emerging metamorphosis.

All things work together for good to them that love God
and for those who are called unto his purpose.
~ Romans 8:28

꒰ *THE EVIDENCE ROOM* ꒱

When one is experiencing what is perceived as a down-spiral in
   life
You need a reference point
A historical reference to transfuse faith
An experience that reminds you that you are not just
   coincidentally on earth, at this time, in this space
But that, indeed, you are here by divine design
The evidence room serves this purpose.
As is the case in the police quarters, there is a room called the
   evidence room
Where all the evidence from the crime scenes is stored
To serve as credible sources of proof or disproof for both sides:
   the prosecution and the defense

For me, my evidence room, my reference of faith, can be found
   in all I've shared.
But, there is yet one, of which you may remain unaware.
There was a car accident that occurred at the age of 16 years,
   three years after my mom died.
I was one of six passengers including the driver in a car,
   traveling from Spanish Town to Linstead, Jamaica destined
   for our usual Sunday morning church service.

But tragically, our car capsized in the river, on a road referred to
in Jamaica, as 'River Road'.
I was one of three passengers who survived.
And I asked God repeatedly...why?
Why did I survive?
Because there's evidence that I could have, and should have,
died
But I was spared for a reason

So, in those moments when debris of doubt slithers its way into
the crevices of my mind
When purpose is questioned, misconstrued or misinterpreted as
platitudes
I stroll down to the evidence room
Where I marvel at the escape of what appeared to be inevitable
doom and gloom
Where the evidence provides the $oul currency
To permanently evict and annihilate doubt, and uphold faith in
purpose
Bridging the path to soul immunity.

ꙮ *THE HUM IN HUMILITY* ꙮ

THE UPSIDE OF DOWN

Moving on to Higher Education
A time for growth, more threshing days
Needless to say
I remained quite 'the odd ball out' at play
Or at least, so to speak ….
There was no anticipation or expectation of an impending social
peak.

So, instead I remained focused, steadfastly planted 'in my lane'
Thus, leaving no propensity for being vain
The $oul currency that I gained

Prepared me for the future I had yet to face
Which would demand much more grace

And, all the milestones on the path to soul immunity
Required a certain prerequisite, and that was, my
humility

You see, with all my accolades
All those awards I've attained
I'll bet you wouldn't believe I could be treated with any disdain
Or, that I could fail at dominating my terrain.

But in truth, I faced much opposition
And learnt the bitter taste of rejection without explanation

Nonetheless, I worked arduously, by not just being clinically
adept
But complemented with passion for the purpose I was called to
fulfill
Walking in his Grace, His guidance and His will.

Here's the $oul Currency
That I gleaned in this restless place:

Snares in every space
Does not preclude giving one's all
Of course, bolstered and strengthened by His Grace
I discovered that rejection by demand leads to redirection
And the building blocks of mental stamina are layered by
resistance from opposition

But the strong emotional foundation
Is not built without mounting frustration
Seething in moments of compounding stress
Likened to what Paul referred to as "a thorn in his flesh"

But even so, after all the long and repetitive sighs
His sufficient Grace was always the answer to the question 'Why'?

Indeed, purpose primed by passion
Is the sweet nectar that neutralizes the bitter taste of rejection
Like the savored honey from the bee
That buzz is the *Hum in Humility*
The crown that reshapes the frown
It's the upside of down.

> *The battles we fight*
> *Are usually not the ones we incite*
> *It's often not the ones we dare*
> *That we ultimately fear*
> *But it's the ones we don't anticipate*
> *The ones that, in truth, to endure we hate*
> *But those are the ones that build our indelible faith*
> *And to that, my friend, there is no debate.*
> ~ Sophia Edwards-Bennett

◎ THE MISSION OF LIGHT ◎

Light is destined to be seen…by 'them'
And therein lies the problem
Because when you have light that emanates
You may find yourself, without warning as the bait
Or the subject of contentious debate
And although that is clearly not your intention
It may be misinterpreted as such, fueled by misinformation

But your light shines, without condition
It has no other mission
It needs no instruction
Neither does it wait for permission
So, when light meets opposition
Or is attacked for its vision
There is only one response regardless of era, culture or time
One option, one goal, one answer comes to mind
That is…shine!
Shine bright in the dark, dim, in any arena of any kind

Just Shine!
Not to humiliate, repudiate or retaliate
But to illuminate
To expose all the hidden sparks in everyone around you
So that their light can shine bright too

I hope that you gained divine insight
Because in any and every circumstance light is light
Indeed, light is $oul currency
To use unselfishly
To help each other along our paths to soul immunity

> *If I say, "Surely the darkness will hide me*
> *and the light become night around me,"*
> *even the darkness will not be dark to you;*
> *the night will shine like the day,*
> *for darkness is as light to you.*
> ~ Psalm 139:11-12

♪ *LIGHT OR ECLIPSE?* ♪

To shine your light
You must avoid an eclipse
So, I would be remiss
If I did not insist
On one thing
And that is that …
Amidst all the travesties and adversities
No matter how much shame, hurt or self-blame
No matter how vitriolic the opposition or piercing the blade of
    pain

There is a $oul currency that is absolutely essential
In any battle, regardless of the platform, mode of transmission,
    nidus or inception
There is an integral currency for your purpose, passion, or
    mission

And it is of paramount importance for your soul immunity
And that is, forgiveness; it is an indispensable $oul Currency.
Not just to be granted to others, but to you, by you, and for you
To gain freedom from bitterness, to release hurt and pain
For where forgiveness is given, $oul currency is gained.

> *But I tell you, love your enemies and*
> *pray for those who persecute you.*
> ~ Matthew 5:44

◎ **FORGIVENESS** ◎

An Essential $oul Currency on the Path to Soul Immunity

Recently I had an encounter
Which led me to extend my thoughts to the pervasive cancel
culture
How we so quickly shine the light on the errors
The mishaps, mistakes or misstep of others
It is true that whether conscious or subconsciously
We all harbor the propensity
To wed ourselves to our own creeds and proclivities
Which creates a web of an intricate grid, impermeable to other
dogmas or their credibilities
So I thought it imperative
To dutifully transpose to the foreground, our own fallibilities
So that we may not just reflexively
Analyze others microscopically
Or blatantly magnify aberrant nature of our kindred or
counterparts' actions or attitudes

Because until we can adopt the ability to see ourselves as
carriers of genetic traits with different, but nonetheless
irrefutable affinity to some fallibility
We cannot, and ultimately will not, accept in a nonjudgmental
fashion dissimilar cultures, tendencies, capabilities or abilities

To this end, I decided to first compose a prose about fallibility,
as a dovetail to this commentary, and serve as a preface to the
ensuing prose that proclaims the healing power of forgiveness
Because the acknowledgement of our own fallibility precedes
not only the forgiveness of ourselves, but that of others
And their inabilities to meet our expectations or aptitudes or
innate capacities.

As a disclaimer, I am in no way sanctioning mediocrity
And this exposition, is certainly not to be interpreted as homily
But it is only to revisit a discourse, to awaken in us an
awareness of our own fallibility
So that we can ascribe forgiveness as not only a vital, but
powerful $oul currency
Because in my own self-discovery
I had an epiphany

That unforgiveness is a soul malignancy
An invasive psychological cancer that I had developed from all
my experiences of denigration, opposition, and rejection
But the ablation of this imminent morbidity
Required emotional nimbleness and unabashed humility
To gain healing that was acutely and chronically necessary
To forgive every contributing source to the difficulty of my
course
In order to gain $oul Currency
On my path to soul immunity.

♩ *THE INFALLIBLE TRUTH* ♪

Is that we are all fallible
That is, we all make mistakes
Whether or not we are held accountable
Whether intentional or projected as statistically probable
It is simply a human propensity that is inevitable
So what's the point of this penned prose other than being
recitable?

Well, it's certainly not to excuse or recuse the inexplicable
Or to condemn the prosecutors or accusers of the so often
　　estranged unforgivable
But it's to define our perspective
The first step of which is self-examination and micro-detection
With deep introspection
And for that we all need a proverbial mirror
To stare face to face at our own error
Our imperfect histories and all our instances of fallibility
And, after a few decades on earth, if your list can be deferred
Then the story of His Grace has not been fully heard
But my conjecture is that if your list is as endless as mine
If you can admit, that it is not pristine, pure or divine
Then we're standing resolute in the shadow of the truth of many
　　lifetimes

Now, allow me to explicate
That to be abstruse is not the goal of this expatriate

It's not meant to absolve anyone's guilt of executing crime
Or the contrary, to adjudicate, reprimand or pronounce
　　abdication of any kind

But it is to call to our attention the intentions of our decisions
Whenever we cast blame, judgement or condemnation without
　　much consideration
To see the reflection of our own vulnerabilities, known or
　　hidden infractions
Whether blatant or subtle, dormant or flamboyant
It's a call to the cause
To mentally pause,
Then sincerely, without hypocrisy and with complete
　　transparency

Evaluate others on the same moral, ethical scale and integral
　　intensity, as we would ourselves

And, if we can imagine congruent, similar narratives or life
    circumstances
Then delve deeply
Into our hearts' well of forgiveness, compassion and sensitivity.
Only then can we truly say, with unequivocal credibility and
    authenticity
That we treat, value, evaluate and formulate conclusions about,
    each other, as we do ourselves, sincerely, consistently and
    without hypocrisy.
That is, and will reveal, most endearingly, the infallible truth in
    all our fallibility.

⟩ *THE HEALING IN FORGIVENESS* ⟨

When we feel pain
Our nature is to ascribe blame
To absolve ourselves of the same

And in doing so
We feel the compelling need to assign a foe
But how do any of these actions heal our pain?

Deep down we're aware that they don't
But they somehow corroborate that you're sane
That your pain is real, as you express effusively how you feel
So it provides self-vindication and self-image preservation
And yes, it's self-soothing
But, as effective as it may seem
The truth is that real healing, lies somewhere in between
Because you can assign blame if someone inflicts pain, acts
    toward you with disdain, maligns, and anathema circulates

But once you accept the reality of what's in real time occurring
The next bold step is to, without exclusivity, analyze your true
    feelings

All, not some, because that is what is unquestionably required
    for your healing
And in this phase of the dissection of one's heart, with deep
    introspection
Identifying your role, however small, even if your acts were
    with good intention
Leave room in your consideration for mutual misinterpretation

Then the last step is a simple decision
Decide what you have learnt, from one's self-interrogation
Now here's what I've learnt from my open-heart surgical
    exploration
Emotional ischemic attacks suffered from others selfish
    grievances or malicious intentions
In time, with time, and in the tests of time
I grew in wisdom, inner strength and humility
I learnt how to heal in 'the in-between'

And so, even though the acute pain and the enduring process
    seem unbearable
In the end, there are so many intangibles that are attainable

Because on, and in the journey, you discover bruises and
    wounds, though seemingly unrelated
Those that you either intentionally or subconsciously buried
    deep inside, undetected
 Or those you thought were forgotten, and thus remained
    neglected
Are all brought to the surface, and fortuitously subjected
To the healing that they too, so desperately needed

So you see…
It is indeed, such a rewarding process
That after successive doses of forgiveness
You no longer wear the garment of bitterness
But instead, clothed with the lessons from your experiences
The deep well of wisdom,
The wealth of knowledge you gleaned

To which you now have access
Along with the strength you now possess
All serve as a compass
To instruct, to guide, to lead you on the path to…
Not reticent, but unprompted, unabashed, sincere and
   wholehearted forgiveness.

Furthermore, Romans 12:19 states clearly:
'Vengeance is mine,' saith the Lord, 'I will repay.'

He who created Heaven and Earth, placed the stars in the sky
   And they never cease to obey
He's in control
No matter how powerful someone's title or roll
However prosperous your opposition may appear
While you're hurting and in deep despair
Do not allow what you can see around you to distract you or
   grieve your soul

In His words: 'do not be anxious'
Because He's in control
So release it all, as your story unfolds
For forgiveness is brave; and to forgive is bold.

◎ FINAL THOUGHTS ABOUT MY JOURNEY ◎

My Path to Soul Immunity

It's interesting, life that is…
And ever so unpredictable
Hindsight, after all, is 20/20
Otherwise referred to as insight
Skill sets I never thought I'd use
Spelling bees, speech festivals, all the grammar
And the golden rules
In the short span of 13 years

My Mom, Mummy, taught me all these tools
Little did I know, that in decades to come I'd see
That this was also 'currency'
To be dispensed, deposited, exchanged in all its potency
In a future, an Aeon that she did not live to actually see
My path to soul immunity.

So, you may ask ...
What's the lesson in this Dr. EB?
Here's what I see
Life is a maze
Difficult to maneuver in its incumbent haze
Wherein, the pieces of the puzzle are arranged unpredictably
So, the pieces don't fit as desired, temporally
That is to say, the pieces that fit, often don't present
    consecutively
But ultimately, they all appear, and on time
In your life, and in mine
If you look closely
Observe keenly
And lean in intentionally

So stay focused
Veer straight ahead
And even if along your path you look to the left or to the right
Always keep your goal, your purpose, your destiny in sight

Clothe yourself with authenticity
Whether triumphant, or in times of adversity
And yes, admittedly
Adversity is always perched on the precipice of pain
But your pain should not be endured in vain.
That is to say:
It should never be wasted but instead harnessed to yield gain.

And from these experiences you will attain
As a corollary, life's extract of sobriety
Ultimately, to draw from your well of wisdom

Taste from your table of truth
Seasoned with an attitude of gratitude
Replenished by the fountain of Faith
Grounded in His grace.
For your path is yours, and yours alone
Your path my friend, cannot be cloned
There will be obstacles, I have no doubt
From those with clout, and those without

But hurdles do not present to elicit pout
But instead, the purpose is to reveal what you're really about...
Strength, courage and tenacity
To live, to dream, to share all your God-given gifts and every
    idiosyncrasy
To shine your light, even throughout the hurt and pain
Your brilliant spark on this earth must remain
Because it's only then that we will partake, and gain the $oul
    Currency
That led to your path to Soul Immunity.

So now...
I've revealed an excerpt of my path, that led to my $oul
    currency
To help you to identify yours, hopefully,
So that you can find your path to Soul Immunity.

One More Prose Before I Go

Before I go, I must pay tribute and gratitude to those who I refer
    to as the Divine, Disguised, and Dispatched.
Because without them it would be nearly impossible for me and
    for you
To overcome those periods in life when there seemed to be no-
    one to call on, no one to advise you what to do...

So here goes my last prose of *Part B* entitled: The Divine
    Ecosystem

ℜ *THE DIVINE ECOSYSTEM* ℭ

The timing is so well ordained

You couldn't have planned it, by willful decision or argued
  vehemently against it without refrain

But it's only after mulling, in retrospect
And upon pensive review, that we realize that to the
  millisecond, the sequence was nothing short of perfect

You may surmise, that it's the favorable life events that herein I
  describe
Or the positive moments to which I refer
But to the painful and traumatic experiences I also defer
Because, though acts and occurrences in life's mazed corridors
May seem so random and ostensibly out of order
Upon distillation, we gain revelation that they are sourced by
  the divine progenitor
Whom to, and with no-one, He (the omniscient) needs to confer
Because, you see, He orchestrates our life's symphony with
  impeccable rhythm
In a realm I've coined *The Divine Ecosystem*
Yes, you've heard me refer to the Divine, Disguised and
  Dispatched
In interviews, or in written or other spoken debuts
Or other interactive forums that I pursue

The Divine, Disguised, and Dispatched
are those people, unrelated, initially appearing seemingly
detached
Distant from anyone we deliberately gravitate toward or become
  emotionally attached
But they enter our lives without announcement, or the highlight
  of a breaking news flash

And surprisingly and refreshingly-they make such an indelible,
  deeply-embedded impact
That at times it may seem incredible or ineffable, in fact
I myself have a virtuous list to propose
Too many to enclose in this expository prose
But a few from my memory bank, I do feel compelled to
  disclose
There were the high school teachers who groomed me in
  competitive debate
Those who invariably encouraged, never wavering or doubting a
  fortuitous fate
The friends who, as we say back home, I can count on one hand
Those on whom I could depend no matter what the
  circumstance
It's the mentor who cared genuinely and consequently saw
  'something' in me
That others didn't, or just were not meant to see
And I could go on (and on) incessantly

If you dissect your life's path, I know you will unveil a story or
  two
Where the Divine, Disguised, and Dispatched dismantled
  negative narratives of you
And instead cultivated and stewarded the intangibles you
  imbued
You may have called it coincidence
Or even ascribed it good luck with bold, unrelenting confidence
Or maybe you deemed it good karma or chance
A flip of a coin or pinyin: wǔshī (translation the Chinese lion
  dance)
But I say this, not just for rhetorical radiance
But in fact to proclaim
To any audience, albeit without a platform, or a modicum of
  fame
It's not chance, it's not good luck, and it's certainly not just fate
I stand resolutely by this promulgate
It's the symphonic rhythm

The sermonic rendering of the divine ecosystem
After all, on this earth, an ecosystem, we mortal beings, accept
   as true
So surely, we can believe that heaven has one too
I'll close with this question I pose
Served on a platter of ponder within this prose
Presented to me, and to you too
Who are we Divinely, Disguised and Dispatched to?

⤙ *Preface* ⤚
to
PART C

Bound by *love*, embroidered with *truth*,
sealed with *inspirational prose*

Inspiration for Cancer Patients around the globe
Insight for their loved ones
Institution of The Ministry of Medicine
Inside the Clinic Walls: Sense of Community

From: A Cancer Doctor

My hope is that within these prose
You will find *your $oul Currency:*

- ❀ Love
- ❀ Hope
- ❀ Faith
- ❀ Heart to Heart Transparency expressed effusively
- ❀ The Truth about You (Not you defined by your diagnosis, but the real YOU)
- ❀ Unbridled Admiration
- ❀ Bridge of Understanding
- ❀ Family
- ❀ The Ministry of Medicine
- ❀ Sense of Community
- ❀ Pearls of wisdom from a cancer patient

To guide you on your *unique path to Soul Immunity*
Sincerely,
  Dr. EB ✄

And now abideth Faith, Hope and Love.
But the greatest of these is Love.
~ 1 Corinthians 13:13 NKJV

THE $OUL CURRENCY OF LOVE
(For cancer patients around the globe)
– From me, Dr. EB ⚕

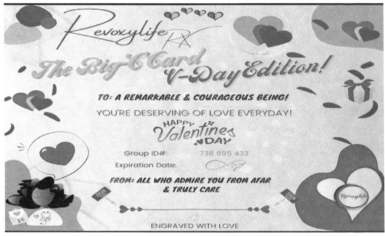

The Big C Card

With Love

Before my exposure to patients
I designed chemotherapy agents
To treat cancer just like the current ones do
Then in my medical training I met you
And with each encounter, my admiration grew
It was then that I knew
My purpose, it's true
I was meant to treat and take care of you

So, this is an expression of love, written for you
With every day in mind
Applied each day, of any kind
No matter where you're from, your accent or ancestral descent
You intrigue us all with your unwavering courage and strength

Your tenacity and zest for life you maintain
Too much to lose, so much to gain

For your future you relentlessly fight
Each day with all your might
And for those you love deeply, you go the extra mile
Seemingly effortlessly, always wearing a smile

You proudly carry your torch of hope
While you teach us all, the true meaning of patience
One day at a time, you navigate with cadence
To appreciate life, the silence in the noise
You dissect the disquietude with so much poise

The vicissitudes throughout treatments you face
Weighing the balance of uncertainty, with so much grace

And because you're so special, indeed remarkable, we'd say
You are deserving of unconditional love, each and every day

So, from all who admire you from afar, and truly care
From your friends, your family, and those you endear

Unwaveringly, this tribute, we all sign.

As we declare from our hearts
That today, and every day
You are indeed remarkable
And that, each day, and at all times
You are a special Valentine

With blessings from above,
Engraved with love
  Dr. EB ✀

⤜ **PART C** ⤛

⤜ *Prologue to Part C* ⤛

The remainder of this book is dedicated to cancer patients and
their loved ones
To delineate a path that can be guided by their unique Soul
currency to the desired destination of Soul Immunity.

So, allow me the honor of presenting to you, this gift
Laced with grace
Bound with love
And embossed in truth
From me – a cancer doctor
To cancer patients, their loved ones, caregivers, and those in the
medical profession around the globe.
We need a cure for cancer, we all concur
But in the meantime, we can…
We need to, we must, create a safe space
An altar of grace
An antidote for our patients' souls, their spirits, their hearts
One does not preclude the other
We can launch both crusades
So that the trepidation, hopelessness, the anxiety, the pain, the
loss of who they were, who they were meant to be, is not the
prevailing narrative of our cancer patients.
To provide a fortress, a path, intercession for:

The process of almost giving up, but not…
Failing but recovering…
Losing but fighting again…
Doubting but believing again
The dark of night waiting for the break of dawn
Weeping, and waiting
Until joy comes in the morning

Step by step
With every breath
Day by day
Come what may
They'll each tell their story
Of a life lived, hope gripped relentlessly
On this earth, where sorrow never ceases
Joy alas, its possibility, it appeases
And through it all, we gained $oul Currency
That my friend, is the path to Soul Immunity.

There's so much more that I could say
But that's another book in the future in play

So here goes *Part C*
The preface, prologue, proses and interludes

And yes – as always – at the end, there's a song
An anthem for our cancer patients around the globe.

It's a song for you, a song for me
A song for everyone who believes it
For everyone who will receive it.

❥ INTERLUDE to DIAGNOSIS ❦

Given the nature of cancer diagnosis, and the clinically-warranted expedience of the ensuing work-up/investigational studies, imaging, laboratory evaluation, our patients do not have adequate time to process their diagnosis emotionally and assimilate, let alone attain at a higher psychological 'rung', before they are thrust into a whirlwind, a cycle of appointments and tests; and subsequent treatments.

One of their myriad of appointments, is with me, the Radiation Oncologist.

It is the acknowledgment of this period, akin to a 'holding pattern'; the unbearable time between the time of diagnosis, multiple scheduled appointments and the long-awaited consultation for a face-to-face discussion that I highlight in the prose. Not just a mere description, but to eavesdrop on 'the inside voice' of both the patient and physician – a louver to the narrative in our minds in that liminal place, time and space.

❧ *THE MANDATORY MEETING OF STRANGERS* ❧

Our paths conceived evitable to cross
But for this unwelcomed intrusion in your life
This diagnosis of the Big C cancer, inserts the unforeseen pause
All still seeming so surreal

As you're thrust into a whirlwind of life's unpredictable
    courtroom
Where it seems there's no appeal
And as you attempt to decipher your thoughts
Within this upheaved mind with anxiety fraught
In a mental tug of war, confused, you find yourself caught

You stare at the door of the refrigerator
Now hosting a very busy saturated calendar
With expanding list of appointments, tests, doctors
It's all so very clustered

Resentment stirs up within, as your promises fade
Dates, times and events
Pledged to family, the endeared and treasured friends
Are steadily erased and replaced by addendums and asterisks
Indicating dates a yonder
Qualified with question marks
Reunions asunder

Allowing your eyes to focus on today's agenda
Highlighted, bolded for emphasis
Is our summoned meeting
What will that entail you wonder
As the many other unknowns you ponder

Indulging in cautious ruminations
Perplexed, perturbed by trepidation
Yet resisting any forecast or predictions

Uncertainties spouting

Arousing within
Mental walls steadily closing in

But you breathe deeply,
Emotions reigned in consciously

You don your mask of bravery
Strutting your steady gait in the direction of clarity

On your way to the expert
To that appointment boldly marked on your calendar
The mandatory meeting with a stranger

That stranger, you see
That doctor is me
I have been consumed with similar thoughts too
Waiting, ever so patiently
To take the very best care of you

Now here we are, in the clinic room
I read your body language, figuratively spelling gloom

I observe your visage, as I explain patiently
Your mind riddled with fear
Nothing I've said seems sufficiently clear

You're frightened, you're sad
This may arguably be the worse day you've ever had

But you listen nonetheless
To the myriad of steps and side effects, albeit perplexed
In the end, you choose to bravely proceed
Forward is at least progress, though admittedly the future is
    uncertain indeed

So you sign consent on the topaz, or on the dotted line
I watch as your loved one reassures you that everything is going
    to be fine.

And while there are no guarantees
One thing's for sure, and that I'll decree

I'll employ all the knowledge, all the tools and my acquired
expertise
And with punctilious attention, my unfailing efforts will never
cease

But with all the spectrum of my acumen, all my talents, I'm just
a human being
But with the weight of His Glory, this earthen vessel has the
power to heal

❧ INTERLUDE to THINKING OF YOU ❦

To convey that it's true: we're thinking of you
For cancer patients and their loved ones too

This version of 'Thinking Of You' (versus that published in my audiobook, *Higher Ground*) is written for you and your 'corner', you and the other slices of your 'life's favorite pie', your spouse, significant other, caretakers, friends, colleagues, admirers and acquaintances.

For those who gravitated toward this book, because of your spouse, family member, or close friend, a colleague or an acquaintance who has been diagnosed with cancer.

Or maybe the person you're thinking of when you peruse this book, is a cancer survivor. But you know that every time he or she is scheduled for a follow up or checkup, whether it's every 3, 4, 6 months or annually, a psychological cycle of anxiety is evoked.

You find yourself not knowing what to say
Because whatever you're thinking to convey
Seems inadequate to allay
All the menacing thoughts that plague them on that, or any
   given day

So, I composed
This insightful prose
Just for you

To curate your thoughts
To assay all the emotions at play
To convey all the thoughts you could not, did not, or may not
   say…

And *to you, cancer patients*,
Indeed, heroes around the globe

So that you'll see, all that we see in you
So that you will know
When we say you are indeed remarkable,
It's unequivocally true
And we are, sincerely, thinking of you.

From: **All of us**
To: **All of you**

) *THINKING OF YOU* (

for Cancer Patients

A cliche used almost ubiquitously
A phrase of endearment, sometimes addended glibly
Often embossed on greeting cards or memorabilia
With kind thoughts to share
Affection, and to evince care
Whether ported from a distance, or from its origin near

Thinking of you is...
The quintessence of thoughtful resort
Safe and simple, seldom met with retort

But this, herein, is not just a task
Effaced with rhetorical mask

It's authentic, it's profound, and it's sincere
Breaching the shield of fear
Reaching the soul's depth; what lies beneath to probe
All within this insightful prose
For cancer patients around the globe

This is the principle of how; the characterization of what; and
    the momentous clarity of when; we think of you
Admittedly, an incomplete summation of our approbation
Limited by the finite descriptors that any language could afford

Nonetheless, parenthesized by our perceptional accord

Your thoughts of the future clouded with uncertainty
Misted with its inherent unpredictability

Entangled with a panoply of smears and restless tears
Yet despite the pain, frustration, doubts and fear
Life you still bravely dare
Boldly proclaiming 'I'm still here'
And though you may have thoughts of giving up
Sometimes, decidedly without bluff
Self-martyred by your inner dissonance and pain
Threatening the future for which you were ordained

But these psychological dents
Do not negate your strengths

And scars borne from the deep wounds of emotional solitude
Could never alter, defeat or preclude
Your incredible fortitude

But in fact, they authenticate your exceptional capacity
To rebound on the 'rim' of faith, with such tenacity
Indeed, a remarkable attribute
Might I say, that's just one of many irrefutable truths

So, whenever you're harboring thoughts of uncertainty
Or find yourself tethering on the ledge of negativity
When your inner voice declines admiration, defiantly

Just remember this:
Your loved ones, family, physicians unanimously derived
    consensus
You are a flagship, sailing through life's raging seas, though
    petulant and tempestuous
A pioneer of undeniable courage, strength, and indubitable
    resilience

An emblem of all these admirable attributes combined –a
   human nexus
Yes, that's you …

That's the 'you' we see, as clear as can be
However, whatever, and whenever we're thinking of you

And, if you take a good, long, thoughtful look at yourself and
   all that you've been through
That true version of you
You'll see it too

❥ INTERLUDE to UNDERSTANDING ❦

Even if unmet, unknown, or existing in anonymity

Or your idiosyncrasies cannot be described explicably

You should be understood just as you are, uniquely

Your voice heard, distinctly

And your journey acknowledged, wholeheartedly

So herein is a **bridge of understanding**

Not for catechizing

But to serve as a conduit of explicit communication

For your consideration

♪ *BRIDGE OF UNDERSTANDING* ♪

An explication, to mitigate misinterpretation and foster
   connectivity
Promote peace and hope, holstered in unity.

This bridge of understanding serves as an aqueduct to those
   close, the reason you're mercurial at times, although that's not
   your intended goal

That your occasional outbursts underscore your despise
   for your sudden loss, and lack of control
Of your world mutating so rapidly right before your very eyes

Why without thinking, you may bellow with sharp words,
   cutting like a knife
As you wrestle with the fact that you never consented to this
   chapter of your life.

This bridge is for those days when you feel your body has
   betrayed you without warning
Or when you're so weak, life has completely zapped all your
   energy
And you're left in dire need of sustainability

When the tears rain, smearing the reflection of your beauty and
   light
The *bridge* forecasts dawn – daylight in sight

It speaks peace to the warfare in your mind
And redirects your eyes to the end of the tunnel, where there's a
   flicker of light – a sign of hope you'll find

When life seeks to subterfuge your mind of memorable repute
The bridge unfolds the scroll of better times, and life's indelible
   truths

The bridge can sit with you in silence, if that's your desire
And without speaking, hearts converse, until to rest you retire

Hoping for dreams with prescient pleasures of a better
   tomorrow
Where bliss and peace collide, and courses alter
Leading to a safe path, traversed without falter
Like a bridge, perched over troubled water

❥ INTERLUDE to RE-ATTITUDES ❦

In my recent Audio Book entitled *'Higher Ground'* I highlight the seven (7) Big C *Re*-attitudes developed to address the psychological toxicities; to brigade against the psychological seige, induced by the diagnosis of the Big-C (cancer). They are:

> ***Re****storation of Hope*
> ***Re****clamation of Identity*
> ***Re****affirmation of Self-Worth*
> ***Re****-appraisal of Life*
> ***Re****quited Admiration*
> ***Re****habilitation of the Mind*
> ***Re****-ignition of Purpose*

The ***'Re'*** - represents the enactment/the attainment.
The specified attitude connotes the desired and attainable element of one's inner spirit.

These seven (7) elements can be sequestered, commissioned and suffused under the canopy of *The Ministry of Medicine.*

The acronym **HIS LAMP** denotes the attainable and restorable attributes:

H*ope,* ***I****dentity,* ***S****elf-Worth,* ***L****ife,* ***A****dmiration,* ***M****ind,* ***P****urpose*

One of the Big C *Re*-attitudes is the *Restoration of Hope*

The following prose is written to incise and drain the abscess of hopelessness that can arrest cancer patients and offer healing with hope, as a $oul Currency, on a path to Soul Immunity.

♪ *HOPE* ♪
for Cancer Patients

Biblically, it is expressed as a rhetoric of faith
That to wit, there is no debate

It is the interceding reset chime
That disrupts the relay of repression in your mind

In succession
Hope gnaws at the links in the chain of depression

When the walls are closing in, alone in the dark
It's the flicker that forecasts an impending spark
When you've acceded to seemingly immutable emptiness
It's the voice that speaks in the silence of your loneliness

Hope is:
The sound that echoes your thoughts audibly
Awakening your subconscious to an alternate reality

The voice that beckons to you
'Look closely'
'Listen keenly'
'Search within, deeply'
Yes, it's that still small voice
That pierces through the eerie noise

Rising in combat, to fight your fears
Reinforcing the promise of seers
That even in the midst of your tears

Hope, it lingers near

So wait my friend, just a little while longer
There's still the fourth quarter
Hang on, till dawn

For hope sees beyond the veil of darkness
Hope to live
Hope to give

Hope to receive
Hope to believe

Hope peers through the lens of your soul
To reveal your truth
Your story to unfold

❥ INTERLUDE to FAITH ❦

Now, since
'Faith is the substance of things hoped for,
the evidence of things not seen.'
~ Hebrews 11:1

♪ *REST AWAITS ON PILLOWS OF FAITH* ♪
for Cancer Patients

I'll confess
The truth I must relay
That there are times when, to the place of fear, I drift at bay
Where tides of doubt my mind replays
But I linger not, in that dark and lonely place
Because I'm summoned by the voice of grace

I know not what the future holds
But I'll know more, as time unfolds

I'm just a vessel, clay in the Potter's hands
In Him I'll place my life, my hopes, my dreams
And all of my best-laid plans

The Big C, daunting and scary as it might be
Strength and courage, without repeal, He has granted to me
So the final say, is His to decree

So as I live and breathe, this life I'll treasure
My beautiful family, friends, so closely tethered
And all of life's simple pleasures
The value of which is too great to measure

So, without further ado
I'll live each day in gratitude to **YOU**

Wisdom earned from my sojourn I'll share
With my neighbors, those I know not, and those I hold dear

To impart knowledge, a guiding light
From the first to the fourth watch of the night
And when sadness hovers
I'll always remember
My heart is adorned with your love that completely covers

To the secure warm blankets of hope
Troubled souls can elope

Faces buried in sheets of peace
Humbly postured, on bended knees

Heavenly hands embrace
In that serene, peaceful place

Fretful minds to abate
Surrendering my fate
To the only one who has the power to dictate

So to His voice I heed
Because in Him I believe
And, with that said
I'll rest my head
On the pillows of faith.

❧ INTERLUDE to SARA ☙

I've included this chapter about my late patient Sara, to share with you lessons learnt from her sojourn.

After all, an experiential nexus creates a synergistic harvest that yields fruits of knowledge to impart to others; but also seeds of concepts to be planted, nourished, and grown.

Without reservation, I know that Sara would gain much fulfillment from the implicit didactic extracts from her journey; and the unquantifiable assets of relatability.

And, if the lessons presented and learnt herein, are not temporally applicable for this moment in time, they can augment our inventory of preparatory psychological tools.

So that, at some time in the future, to which we are not yet privy, we can retrieve these skill sets from our reservoir, when its application is essential, and its intervention is, not only prudent, but in fact, critical.

𝄞 *LESSONS FROM SARA* 𝄢

I met Sara as a patient in South Dakota
Our first encounter was, although not easily assigned an
   emotional quotient, would be etched in our cognitive recesses.
Not upon reflection, in retrospect or after deep introspection
But without question, upon first impression.

I recalled that Sara was accompanied by her husband Steven for
   her first consultation
By their body language, visage and energy
I could surmise that, together, they had weathered many
   vicissitudinous seasons

As I explained in detail the role and rationale of palliative
   radiation, offering no chance of cure.
They expressed their understanding and appreciation of the
   contents of our discussion.

When we entered the question phase
Steven took the 'reins' in Sara's place
Not because she couldn't, but simply because she chose not to,
   and thus didn't…

You see, Sara was laconic, a keen listener
And an even keener observer
So, I wasn't misled that he spoke in her stead

And, when she chose to speak, or pose questions, she was
   definitive and direct
Not intimating reticence to proceed
No, not at all
That was not her intention
But more-so, to carefully dissect the information before its
   consumption and subsequent psychological digestion

I subsequently met with Sara in weekly clinic status-checks
   during her course of treatment

Her eyes, as usual, shuffled with a rhythmic pace
A cyclic display of her gaze
Eyes dancing around the room, alternating with lulls of
intermittent focused attention; simulating a version of musical
chairs

Complimenting her laconic nature
Was her deliberate delivery in conversations
And yet, our connection persisted

At the end of one of our weekly scheduled meetings
I expressed these exact words: *'I see you'*
To which she reacted with non-verbal response
But her visage portrayed that she believed that the words she
heard were true.
I saw her heart, a storage of love, and the kindness she imbued

It was during her usual treatment visits that she shared with me,
one of her hidden talents
Her incredibly adept skills at designing beautifully crafted
edible shoes
And with that, were so many other clues
Of her ingenuity
All harbored in secrecy

At the end of her treatment course
She surprised me with a special gift—sixteen (16) of her most
beautiful, artfully crafted and ever so elegantly adorned
Indeed, I was flattered and honored, yet humbled
My heart nestled in warm appreciation

A few months after my last encounter with Sara
While I was practicing at another cancer center
Unexpected, breaking the ambient, humming sound of the air
conditioning unit in the background of my office, the phone
rang.

I recall distinctly, it was a Monday morning, August 31, 2020.
At first, I didn't recognize the voice on the other side.
But my ignorance was ephemeral.
It was Steven, Sara's husband. He called to inform me that Sara
had passed the day prior, Sunday August 30th, 2020.

The sadness, the loss, the pain, the grief
Were all so very palpable in his voice
Reaching across states virtually
I could feel the emptiness, the gaping hole he harbored inside.
I effusively conveyed my heartfelt condolences for his loss.

Then, he responded with a statement I did not anticipate.
In his words, and I quote, "I called you because Sara wanted
    you to know how much you meant to her."
My heart was saddened, yet warmed synchronously
By the spoken words, expression of appreciation, delivered on
    Sara's behalf, posthumously.

But, as I exhaled, there was a catechizing peace
Neutralizing the wave of the sadness, though mourning hearts
    did not cease
I sensed Steven's alignment with this knowing, calm
    reassurance as well, albeit tempered with sorrow.
His conviction to honor Sara's desire, coupled with his
    vulnerability, was authentic, solemn, and admirable.

I was truly honored, and humbled, by Sara's thoughts of
    endearment relayed by Steven

Indeed, it was an attestation and affirmation that impactful
    encounters and invested time with our patients
Leaning in, to treat the whole patient, not isolating or
    compartmentalizing
Invades beyond the shielding walls of anxiety and fears
Comforts and reassures, leaving a residue of indelible thoughts
    of genuine care.

The following prose speaks to the referenced attestation of indelible endearment

As a tribute to Sara, it is aptly entitled: *I SEE YOU*

ॐ *I SEE YOU* ॐ

When we meet our patients, they present with more than just
    their diagnosis
They come packaged neatly or disheveled
The pain of the past coupled with the shock and fear of what's
    at hand
Their journey, what their lives entailed prior to their diagnosis,
    and its culmination to the present time
With all their emotions, like a complex matrix
intertwined

These are the stories of their lives
The ones with which our hearts jive
The details they share
Echoing from their deepest fear
Their close connections
The lingering regretful reflections
And unpleasant repercussions
That plague their thoughts, derail their plans
And evict all their dreams; begrudgingly ripping control from
    their hands

The memory of Sara and my conversations
with her family, and all my patient encounters and lessons
    pursuant
Was a ratification of sorts, of the panoply of interconnected
    retrospective inquisitions and realizations.

That is: Formality does not define
Professionalism of any kind

For, the human interaction, in its geniality
Is, indeed, the centerpiece of connectivity
Flanked by the healing tripod of the
The mind, body and the soul
Thus, moving forward
Breaking the mold
Let this be from our vantage
An enlightened, renewed point of view
The modus operandi of the majority
Not just a few
So that in our encounters
We too, can with all sincerity
Say these three (3) powerful words endearingly
"I see you"

◎ <u>DESTINY ENCOUNTERS</u> ◎

What are your thoughts?

Having treated and/or advised thousands of patients in many different countries, and in different cities and states here in the USA, I've grappled with, and cerebrally explored, the experiential concept of destiny deployment.

Upon reflection on my consequential interactions with my patients originating from so many different backgrounds, creeds, cultures, ethnicities and epochs; questions prompted, stirred in the milieu of thoughts in my mind.

One wonders why them, why me, why you, why now?

Do our unique idiosyncrasies till fertile soil for communication, connectivity and fealty?

Is there an impartation, maybe seemingly insignificant, that is meant to be channeled through our conclave?

Or is there a profound lesson, learnt existentially that we're commissioned to receive?

I thought deeply about the possibility of these 'destiny meetings' and all the proposed questions herein; my rekindled impetus being the series of events that surrounded my meeting with Sara, our bond, my interactions with her family thereafter, because of this strong bond; even in her physical absence on planet earth.

A bond, not forced, not concocted, that could not be strategically pre-planned or consorted; it is a natural gravitation that can only be elicited by spiritual or divine alignment.

The blessing, the wisdom, the reassurance, deep-seated hope that encamped around 'the circle of Sara' was instructive and cathartic.
Can you, can I, can we, entertain the possibility of a similar chain of connection for you, your family, loved ones, and your cancer doctor; if and where destiny abounds?

Because it is there, in that uniquely designed mental architecture, that the human spirit and mind are elevated above the background noise and our corporal frequencies, in that realm where our finite cerebral capacities cannot control, contain or attain.

Below, is an original prose on the subject of Destiny.
Because one's ordained destiny includes *a path to Soul Immunity*.

DESTINY ENCOUNTERS

♪ *MY THOUGHTS* ♪

I've said this before, a statement of conviction
But may I submit, for your earnest consideration
The proclivities, or the dogmas to which our minds cling
   without reservation
The meeting of our soul mates

Our new dream job, we credit without hesitation to destiny, or
    purport as fate
So, here's a question, for your pontification, colloquy or ponder
Is it possible, that your referred physician or medical
    practitioner
Could be more significant than a matter of clinical coincidence,
    or salience?
Could you conceive in your minds that maybe, just maybe,
    there's divine sequence?

Details taken for granted – the timing, location and place of
    residence,
Our current decisions and prior life events
Usher us, all parties of pertinence

To this unforeseen emotional collision, temporal staged
    occurrence or life event

Well, as for me, it's a statement of purpose
In a world that can sometimes seem like an entropic circus
I believe, there are indeed, divinely scheduled appointments in
    this realm of our existence

One that earth, having no knowledge or prescience
Could not surrender or assent
And you, or I, were not granted the option to disagree or dissent
But in perpetuity, this movie of our lives was set in motion
    without our consent

So, with our credits displayed and steadily rolling
Let these words be consoling

Before you or I were born or even entered our mother's womb,
    there was a divine plan
For each and everyone of us, every girl, every boy, every
    woman and man
And yes, it's daunting, and some life events lack reasoning or
    logic

That I myself must confess that I can't profess to understand
But here's what I do; and I hope you can too
I trust in Him, the omniscient one
And, challenged on any witness stand
I'd state the same without recant
I trust and I believe that it's all in the Master's Hand.

⟩ $OUL CURRENCY ⟨

Of The Ministry Of Medicine for Medical Professionals

In the profession of medicine
There are certain unspoken rules
I speak not singularly of the formal profession,
But the actual act of the practice and execution thereof
What it supports, how it comports
What it maintains, and to what it pertains

Herein is the plain and simple truth:

The profession of medicine is not pristine
Not by any means
But it requires an unselfish posture, an ever-abiding connection
   of human beings
It is a professional field that encapsulates the very essence of
   our mortality
All our idiosyncrasies germane to our tendencies
Our spectrum of attributes that fuel our capacities
The genius of intellectuality
The breadth of creativity
The tenacity of our intentionality
The elasticity of our malleability, our neuroplasticity

So that the conventional milestone is perpetually transposed
   with progress
And tradition lingers less

So when we meet our patients
We are not just introduced to their cancer, diagnosis or disease
But to their tapestry of perspectives
Their present, colored by their past
The future dictated by the unanswered question
'Where do we go from here?'
And it is within that framework of inclusivity, compassion and
    sensitivity
That we must strive to apply our practice of medicine as a
    ministry
Firstly, let's debunk the concept that exceptionalism or notoriety
    in medicine precludes the act or display of empathy
Whether putative, arguable, or revered

In like manner, the practice of medicine should not exclude or
    require the percolation of one's cultural identity
But instead, embrace diversity

And, in the case of spirituality, our soul hosts our beliefs in a
    higher being
Not fleeting, but grounded and held in high esteem

And since we're all human beings
There are more similarities
Than may be apparent phenotypically

So, if the feet were placed in another's shoes
A scenario that could very likely be true
What would you do?
What graciousness would you desire to be granted to you?

So, let's connect beyond the profession and post-nominals
Our script, statistics or masked self-control
Sanitization of this priceless gift of human interaction is not the
    goal

Instead, it's a blessed opportunity to elucidate

Beyond the cancer of the patients we face
The treasured things in life they embrace
Because in the clinic room
Is where we commune
It's where we shed the garment of culture
It's where we declutter from impertinent acts of human nature
And instead focus solely on the solemnness of life
The essence of our existence
This interaction is transcendent
Beyond any preconceived beliefs or notions
Indeed, it summons unparalleled devotion
Face to face in that space
We are desensitized from hues, creeds or race
We form a bond that is one of the purest of mankind
And in those moments in time
There in our microcosm, our silo, in that sacred space
Our thoughts are intertwined
As the preservation of life preoccupies our minds
Where hope, strength and courage are synchronized.

It is this patent, transparent operation and heart distillation
That will breach our patients' walls of doubts and fears
To establish that bond of human connection
It is in that space, that state, that unabashed endearing place
Where we not only lend healing, but indeed healing we too
    receive
That is the ministry of medicine, at least, that's what I believe

❧ INTERLUDE to BRIDGES ❦

In my recent audio book, *Higher Ground*, I delivered a prose, entitled, *The Bridge*. We, the people, act as bridges of understanding for our cancer patients.

This prose presented herein, describes the components of a bridge, and a broad array of many bridges layered to macro-scale, to fortify its foundation, with intersecting matrices to increase connectivity.

It reveals a more intimate transcript, and portrays a more vivid picture of the enactment of many other bridges, interconnecting networking in the intimate setting of a cancer clinic.

These are Bridges to, and for, other bridges – projected on the canvas of life.

On this canvas, that we paint each day
Each stroke, each occurrence
Creates a picture
Framed and textured to narrate a different story
From distinct angles of view

What you may imagine transpiring behind our clinic doors, as a
  solemn recording
Yes, there's pain
Yes, there's loss
Yes, there is disappointment, and indeed there's mourning
There's a vast spectrum of emotions
As our feelings as humans vacillate
But, there's another canvas in this gallery
That I'd like to place on display

This prose focuses on that canvas aptly entitled:

♪ *ON THE OTHER SIDE* ♪

THE TIES THAT BIND $OUL CURRENCY
OF THE SENSE OF COMMUNITY

Each day, in our cancer clinic
What will transpire, admittedly, we cannot predict

But a common theme, unwritten, unspoken
Permeates the clinic rooms
Diffused throughout the chemotherapy bays
Traversing the parallel or maze-designed hallways

And on these preplanned, appointed schedules, yet
   unpredictable days
The mission reigns supreme
Unreserved sacrifices and unconditional care

Like a symbol of safety for boats on the shore
Viewed in plain sight, in the line of vision of the pier

These spaces, places,
Silos of undulating paces
Enriched by hues and shades of faces
Endeared by warm embraces

Doctors in white coats, dressed formally
Some adorned with scrubs, bustling intently

Others scurrying, like the replay of a shuffling dance
At least this is the scenery, your vision captures upon a cursory
   glance

But there's so much more that the eyes can meet
So, to closely observe, I invite you to reserve a seat

Allow me to be your steward, painting this canvas, dynamically
I promise it will be an indelible sight to see

Not at all thespian, these are lives
Real people, just like you and me

You'll see patients, whoever walks in
It does not matter who needs attention
It has no bearing on our reaction

Greeted with a smile
Some known by their *aka*
As they've been 'patrons' for a while

If you shift your gaze
Averting your eyes down the hall to the right
There's another scene that will undoubtedly intrigue your sight

A therapist or two, escorting a patient in a wheelchair to the
    treatment machine
Conversing while strolling
Their attentions locked in, ever so keen and captivating

Now carefully rotate, make an oblique left, you'll see in a
    different hallway
A doctor, leaving a room in the clinic bay
Will certainly pique your observational antennae

That's Dr. John Salter
Beside him is his patient, in synchronized saunter,
 Recounting shared interest, or sports, in friendly banter

And as you observe, you'll see that their visage and body
    language portray
Comfort, reassurance, and camaraderie at play

Now, in the backdrop, moving forth

At an obtuse angle, 100 degrees north
Assimilate the activities of the nurses, fully engaged
Some huddled collaborating at their stations
Others dutifully responding to patients, attentively, answering
   their questions

While some work feverishly in their quarters
Fulfilling patients' requests and doctors' orders

In the maze, at the very end of the corridor
There's a sharp bend, at the east corner
You'll find the dosimetrist, physicist or pharmacist
In deep ponder
Developing, formulating, the best treatment plan
For a patient, I just declared, requires clinical coordination,
   emergently on demand

Should you attempt to systematically assemble snapshots of the
   'behind the scenes' moments described
A static depiction you'll erroneously ascribe
As one cannot accurately or adequately transcribe
The execution, the aggregate focus, diligence, and commitment
Or the transduction of intent, solely for the recipient's
   contentment

Because, in painting any canvas
Each stroke, from beginning to end, is a dynamic transaction
Thus, the spontaneous laughter at the check-in desk
Or the bonding occurring in the waiting room, between several
   patients
Like long lost friends

Exchanging details of their journeys
Are all, transpiring in real time, concurrently

So, if we visualize carefully and deliberately through keen lens
You'll see beyond what is perceived by the optical sense

Because it's the continuous flow throughout each day of these
    events
That carves an image so beautiful it will transcend
Any concept that our minds may harbor, assume or contend

But instead, what you'll glean is a *Monet* of human interactions
Divinely ordained
Delivering with love
Reciprocated, and gracefully maintained

This canvas propagates the ethos that true service does not
    cohabitate with mediocrity
But instead, that the human resilience, courage and strength that
    our patients embody
Must be met with the same, in equanimity

You see
We are all blessed collectively
With a reservoir of precious gifts
Adept to honor, save or give light to someone who's ailing or
    whose life is adrift

But at times, there's a perquisite that we fail to acknowledge or
    recognize
That is:
When we give what we can
Share what we have, extend our expertise, or lend a helping
    hand
We are not left with a deficit
Indeed, and in fact, it's quite the opposite

So, on this canvas
This indelible *Monet*
Like Helices of our DNA
Let's Replicate
All over the globe
Hearts and minds in synchrony
This indomitable, irrepressible spirit of humanity

♪ *THE REASON I SING* ♪

In my last book, *Higher Ground*
I ended with a chant for cancer patients
However, I complete this book with a complementary song
I hope it blesses everyone who lends an ear or two, reads,
    whether one pair of eyes, or a few

But allow me to say, before you do
I know we all have different beliefs, different dogmas or
    governed by different ethos
We also have thoughts about what we don't believe
The absoluteness of the creeds to which we do not subscribe

And at this juncture in our lives, whatever we believe or do
We respect each other's rights to harbor what we deem as false
    or true

For that reason, I boldly speak my truth
That wherever I go, whatever I do, whoever I am or aspire to be
With all my imperfections, my strength and weaknesses, gifts,
    the blessings and callings granted unto me
And I say that, emphatically
All of it, was given to me by the Almighty

And so what I do, the prose I compose, the books I pen,
The patients I treat, and to whom I tender, the presentations I
    render
The procedures I perform, the assessment and plans I
    recommend

If you think that I do anything well, or my consummate skill set
    you extol or commend
All attributes, I impute to the one who is omniscient,
    omnipresent and omnipotent
So in everything I do, I acknowledge Him

Not to disregard the beliefs of you or your kin
But to honor mine
Regardless of circumstances, or the test of times

For this I know is true
He's the reason I breathe
The source of my strength
The inspiration for everything I do

So, whatever powers reign on earth
He is my King
And He is the reason that I sing.

*We are not ashamed of the Gospel of Jesus Christ, for it is the
power of God into Salvation for everyone that believeth.*
~ Romans 1:16

For all cancer patients around the globe
Here's a song written just for you, entitled:

I'm Still Here

Sincerely,
Dr. EB ✹

₹ *I'M STILL HERE* ₹

I was living my life
Making plans that I might
Do all the things I promised myself
Pledged to my family and my friends

Then on that day
I could not think clear
Oh how you caused
My heart to fear

I admit I was so afraid
My hopes and dreams
I'd lose them all
That I would cease
To pursue my call

Then suddenly
Something within me
Bellowed so loud
Resoundingly

And the words that I heard
Were from my heart to me
They said you are here
As strong as can be

Yes it is true
I won't deny
There will be times
That I may cry
It will be hard
Yes it will be hard
And giving up
Will play its card

But the words still echo from my heart
I am still here
As strong as can be
Though I may be weak … physically

My heart, my soul, my mind
Synchronously
They say I'm still here
As strong as can be

So each day I rise
Each breath I take
Tomorrow's daybreak
Sunshine or rain
More faith I will gain

Yes I'm still here
I'll conquer my fear
My heart will sing
Let praises ring
For You are my King

And as long as I'm here
My light will shine
I will give love joy and peace
One day at a time

Yes I'm still here
As strong as can be
Let praises ring
My Savior, my Lord
My God, My King

Yes you're still here
As strong as can be
Your heart will sing
Let praises ring
For He is your King

⋙ EPILOGUE ⋘

SUPPLEMENTAL PROSE

⸝ *THE PEACE IN THE PASSING* ⸜

No-one really knows when, how or why
We just live, knowing that with each day, that time may be nigh
That with each year
With each decade, that day might be near
But until then, we do our best, in the midst of this life, its
    unpredictable storms
With all the unknowns, in all shapes and forms
But there are also those very beautiful things that occur along
    the way
That we tend to forget when overwhelmed with dismay

There were wonderful moments shared
From all those who dearly loved and cared
The unexpected joys of life embraced
Children raised
Milestones met
After years of hard work, endurance and sweat

The smiles that warmed our hearts
The love that could touch so deeply even when miles apart
If you relish all that life brought you
Taught you
That you invested in it

Even when tested; admit it
There's a sweet savor, you can taste it
There's a fragrance, you can smell it
There's an indescribable aura, you can feel it

There's a currency that runs through you
It's electric
But it's not measured in joules
It's much greater, much deeper, much wider

It's seismic
It emanates, it replicates
It appreciates, it cultivates
It captivates, it activates
It reignites the spirit
It renovates the mind
It resuscitates the heart
It rejuvenates the body
It inoculates the soul, to restore, to build, to fortify its immunity

That is the essence, the gift, of $oul currency
Indeed, it is a part of our legacy
We can impart it, we can 'will' it
So, we can all find peace in our passing
In our inevitable mortality.